21st CENTURY LIVES
WORLD CUP FOOTBALLERS

Adam Sutherland

First published in 2010 by Wayland

Wayland
338 Euston Road
London NW1 3BH

Wayland Australia
Level 17/207 Kent Street
Sydney, NSW 2000

Senior editor: Debbie Foy
Designer: Rebecca Painter
Picture researcher: Kate Lockley

Picture Acknowledgments: The author and publisher would like to thank the following for allowing their pictures to be reproduced in this publication: VANDERLEI ALMEIDA/AFP/Getty Images: 9 NICOLAS ASFOURI/AFP/Getty Images: 5 FETHI BELAIDI/AFP/Getty Images: 13 ADRIAN DENNIS/AFP/Getty Images: 10 FRANCK FIFE/AFP/Getty Images: 20 Victor Fraile/Getty Images: 12 Photo by Getty Images for adidas: 16 Paul Giamou/MLS via Getty Images: 4 VALERY HACHE/AFP/Getty Images: 11 TOSHIFUMI KITAMURA/AFP/Getty Images: 18 Alex Livesey/Getty Images: Cover, 15 JOHN MACDOUGALL/AFP/Getty Images: 19 Paolo Nucci/WireImage/Getty Images: 17 Ben Radford/Corbis Sports: 8 Andreas Rentz/Bongarts/Getty Images: 14 MIGUEL ROJO/AFP/Getty Images: 7 JAVIER SORIANO/AFP/Getty Images: Title page, 6 John Varley/Offside: 21

British Library Cataloguing in Publication Data:
Sutherland, Adam.
World Cup footballers. -- (21st century lives)
1. Soccer players--Biography--Juvenile literature.
2. World Cup (Soccer)--Juvenile literature.
I. Title II. Series
796.3'34'0922-dc22

Printed in Slovenia

ISBN: 978 0 7502 62019

Wayland is a division of Hachette Children's Books, an Hachette UK company

www.hachette.co.uk

Contents

Cristiano Ronaldo 4
Kaká 6
Lionel Messi 8
Wayne Rooney 10
Fernando Torres 12
Fabio Cannavaro 14
Zinedine Zidane 16
Ronaldo 18
Pelé 20

Other World Cup Footballers 22
Index 24

Some definitions:

FIFA - Fédération International de Football Association
UEFA - Union of European Football Associations
CONCACAF - Confederation of North, Central American and Caribbean Association Football

Cristiano Ronaldo

Global superstar

Ronaldo on the training ground after his record-breaking transfer to Real Madrid.

"After I joined [Manchester United], the manager asked me what number I'd like. I said 28. But Ferguson said, 'No, you're going to have No 7,' and the famous shirt was a source of motivation. I was forced to live up to such an honour."

Cristiano Ronaldo on following in the footsteps of George Best, Eric Cantona and David Beckham, *The Sun*, 12 April 2007

Full name: Cristiano Ronaldo dos Santos Aveiro

Nickname: Ronnie, Rocket Ronaldo, Cristiano Dior

Date and place of birth: 5 February 1985, Funchal, Madeira, Portugal

Clubs: Sporting Lisbon (Portugal) 2001-2003, Manchester United (England) 2003-2009, Real Madrid (Spain) 2009-present

Position: Winger

Early promise: Ronaldo won his first cap for Portugal in a 1-0 victory over Kazakhstan in August 2003. He was a valuable member of the Euro 2004 squad, scoring twice and being named in the Team of the Tournament. He also represented Portugal at the 2004 Olympics.

World Cup appearances: The second-highest scorer in World Cup 2006 qualifying with seven goals, Ronaldo scored his only World Cup goal to date against Iran with a penalty kick. During the quarter final match against England, an argument with then-Manchester United team mate Wayne Rooney resulted in him missing out on the tournament's Best Young Player award due to a negative email campaign from England fans.

Other international achievements: Captained his country at just 22 in a friendly against Brazil in February 2007. Scored eight goals in Portugal's UEFA Euro 2008 qualifying campaign, and has been regular captain under new manager Carlos Quieroz.

Something you might not know about him: Ronaldo was named after the ex-US President Ronald Reagan – his father's favourite actor.

Become an international: Ronaldo is dedicated to being the best player in the world. He admits to spending more time practising than any other player he knows.

Cristiano Ronaldo is the most expensive footballer in the world. His world record transfer in summer 2009 from Manchester United to Real Madrid cost the Spanish club a massive £80m.

Born in the sleepy town of Funchal, Madeira in Portugal, the youngest of four children, Ronaldo started his career with amateur side Andorinha where his father looked after the kit. At 10, he moved to local club CD Nacional where he was spotted by scouts of Sporting Lisbon, who signed him after a three-day trial.

Ronaldo quickly rose through the ranks at Sporting, playing for the Under-16s, Under-17s, Under-18s, B team and first team all in the same season! He scored two goals on his Sporting Lisbon debut, and in the same year made his first appearance for Portugal in the UEFA Under-17 Championships.

In the summer of 2003, Sporting Lisbon played Manchester United in a friendly match and Ronaldo's performance impressed the United players so much that they urged their manager Alex Ferguson to sign him.

Ronaldo became Manchester United's first Portuguese player when he joined for £12.24m in summer 2003. The same year he won his first senior cap for Portugal. He was the second highest goal scorer in FIFA World Cup 2006 qualifying with seven goals, and scored his only World Cup goal so far with a penalty against Iran.

The big talking point of the 2006 World Cup tournament was Ronaldo's involvement in Wayne Rooney's sending off when Portugal played England in the quarter finals. England fans believed Ronaldo influenced the referee to show Rooney a red card for a foul on one of his Portugal team mates. The backlash from English newspapers and supporters nearly forced Ronaldo to leave the country. But instead, he braved the abuse, won back support, and had three more record-breaking years at Manchester United winning three Premier League titles in a row, the Champions League and personally being awarded FIFA World Player of the Year in 2008.

Ronaldo scored eight goals in qualifying for UEFA Euro 2008, but has been less successful in his team's qualifying campaign for the World Cup in South Africa. No one doubts that the Portuguese hit man can come back to form and help his team out when the big occasion demands it.

The winger uses his speed to go past an opponent in a World Cup 2006 game against Iran.

"It is obvious to everyone that Ronaldo is an unbelievable footballer. He is someone I would pay money to watch."

Lionel Messi, 2009

Kaká

The chosen one

Kaká smiles for the cameras at his first Real Madrid press conference.

"[Breaking my vertebra] changed me in the sense that after the incident, I started doing things with more intensity, more commitment, more love... The truth is that the doctors told me I had been very lucky. I was able to return to football after the accident... and since then, like I said, I do everything with more intensity, a lot more love."

Kaká,
***FIFA World* magazine, 2008**

Name: Ricardo Izecson dos Santos Leite

Nickname: Kaká

Date and place of birth: 22 April 1982, Brasilia, Brazil

Clubs: São Paulo (Brazil) 2001-2003, Milan (Italy) 2003-2009, Real Madrid (Spain) 2009-present

Position: Midfield/playmaker

Early promise: At 19, Kaká was called up for the 2001 FIFA World Youth Championships. He made his debut for the senior team in a friendly against Bolivia in January 2002. He was captain for the 2003 CONCACAF Gold Cup where Brazil competed with their Under-23 team, finishing runners-up to Mexico.

World Cup appearances: Kaká was a member of the 2002 FIFA World Cup-winning squad but played only 18 minutes in the tournament. He started his first World Cup Finals match in 2006 and scored his first goal in a 1-0 win over Croatia. Brazil were knocked out in the quarter finals by France.

Other international achievements: A member of the Brazilian squad for the 2005 Confederations Cup, Kaká appeared in all five games and scored once in a 4-1 win over Argentina in the final. He played again in the 2009 Confederations Cup, scoring twice in the group stages against Egypt. He received the Golden Ball for Player of the Tournament, and was named Man of the Match in the 3-2 final win against USA.

Something you might not know about him: Kaká's younger brother gave him the nickname because he couldn't pronounce 'Ricardo'.

Become an international: Kaká has the speed to outrun opponents, the skill to make defence-splitting passes, and the technique and power to score regularly from outside the penalty area.

A devout Christian, Kaká points to the sky after scoring against Uruguay in World Cup 2010 qualifying.

When he scores a goal he points to the sky to say thanks to God, and he has the words 'God is faithful' stitched on his football boots. Off the pitch he is a member of the Atletas de Cristo ('Athletes of Christ') and gives one tenth of his yearly salary to the Brazilian Church. Since 2004 he has been an Ambassador Against Hunger for the United Nations' World Food Programme.

Kaká is called the most influential 'playmaker' (goal scorer and goal provider) in football, and is regularly compared to Diego Maradona. His first season in Italy with Milan he won the Scudetto (the Italian league title) and three years later won the UEFA Champions League. At the final whistle, Kaká took off his Milan shirt and showed a T-shirt that said 'I belong to Jesus'.

Kaká's World Cup experience so far has been limited. He was part of Brazil's 2002 World Cup-winning squad, but only played one game as a substitute against Costa Rica in the first round. In 2006 he scored his first World Cup goal in Brazil's 1-0 win against Croatia in their first group game and was named Man of the Match. In the 2010 qualifying rounds he has been Brazil's second top scorer, helping his team to the top of the South American qualifying group. Kaká is sure to make World Cup 2010 a tournament to remember.

Kaká is not a typical footballer. Unlike many Brazilian players, he grew up in a financially secure family, and divided his time between school and football. Kaká chose football as a career (he could have been a professional tennis player) and signed his first professional contract with São Paulo at 15.

When he was 18, he dived into his grandparents' swimming pool and broke a vertebra (a bone in his back). Doctors told him he might never walk normally again, let alone play football. But Kaká put his faith in God, never gave up believing, and made a full recovery. The following year he made his first team debut for São Paulo, and scored 22 goals in 49 games.

Kaká is different both on and off the pitch. As a footballer, he combines the ball control and eye-catching skills of South American players with the strength and determination of the Europeans.

"Kaká isn't the new Pelé, he is the new Johan Cruyff. He keeps getting better and is so fast. He sees the goal early and when he sets off from midfield he is unique."

Pelé, *The Sun*, 21 May 2007

Lionel Messi

The little genius

Messi lines up for Argentina before a friendly against France.

"I have incredible fun whenever I play, and sometimes I honestly forget it is my job. When I have the ball at my feet, I forget the rest of the world exists. It is the ultimate escape and such an amazing feeling."

Lionel Messi,
***Shortlist* magazine, 2009**

Name: Lionel Andrés Messi

Nickname: The Flea, Messidona

Date and place of birth: 24 June 1987, Rosario, Argentina

Clubs: FC Barcelona (Spain) 2003-present

Position: Winger

Early promise: Messi made his international debut for Argentina Under-20s in June 2004, and won the FIFA World Youth Cup in the following year. He was the star of the tournament, winning the Golden Ball for Best Player, and the Golden Boot for Top Scorer with six goals. He made his debut for the senior side at the age of 18.

World Cup appearances: Messi's only World Cup to date was not a true reflection of his skill. Injured before the tournament, the winger often only started games from the subs' bench. Nevertheless, he became the youngest player to represent Argentina at a World Cup when he came on in the 74th minute against Serbia, and scored the final goal in a 6-0 victory, making him the youngest scorer in the tournament.

Other international achievements: Messi reached the final of the 2007 Copa América, losing 3-0 to Brazil. He won a gold medal with Argentina in the 2008 Beijing Olympics, defeating Nigeria in the final.

Something you might not know about him: Messi is the face of the popular video games Pro Evolution Soccer (PES) 2009 and 2010.

Become an international: Messi is an expert at 'la gambeta' – a high-speed dribble around defenders, made famous by Diego Maradona!

Small and fast, Messi steals the ball from two Mexican players during a 2007 international match.

He quickly rose through the ranks of the club's youth teams and made his debut for the senior Barcelona side in October 2004 at just 17. In the 2006-2007 season Messi really found his feet, scoring 14 goals in just 26 appearances. In the following year he scored an incredible 38 goals and helped his team with the treble of the Spanish league, Spanish cup and UEFA Champions League. The young winger has recently signed a contract extension with Barcelona until 2016.

Messi is now a Spanish citizen, and was offered the chance to play for Spain but instead chose to represent the country where he was born. Nicknamed 'Messidona' because of his similarities to Argentina's football legend Diego Maradona, Messi was the star player of the 2005 FIFA World Youth Championship. He now wears Maradona's number 10 shirt for the senior side, and is his team's source of inspiration. He is Argentina's leading goal scorer in World Cup 2010 qualification and has started every game. Football fans around the world can't wait to see Messi in South Africa.

Lionel Messi is fast, skilful, good with both feet and deadly in front of goal. He is the sort of player all football fans love to watch. Even at seven, he was winning over supporters. On his first day at school, he was excluded from the playground game of football because he was so small. He took to the pitch anyway and dribbled so brilliantly that he was first choice from then on.

At just 13 years old, Messi and his family moved 6,500 miles from his hometown of Rosario in Argentina to Barcelona in Spain. Barcelona scouts had seen him playing for local team Newell's Old Boys and signed him up for their youth development programme. They also offered to pay his medical bills for treatment on a growth hormone deficiency that Messi's family could never have afforded themselves. Thanks to the £500-per-month growth hormone treatment, Messi grew to his current height of 5ft 7in. Without this medical treatment, he was told he would not grow to be taller than 4ft 7in.

"I have seen the player who will inherit my place in Argentine football and his name is Messi. He's a leader and is offering lessons in beautiful football. He has something different to any other player in the world."

Diego Maradona, talking to the BBC, February 2006

Wayne Rooney

Leading from the front

Rooney is hoping to be England's star striker at World Cup 2010.

"As a footballer you want to be the best and I'm no different. It would be nice to be the main man, but for me the team is the most important thing."

Wayne Rooney to the *Daily Mirror*, October 2009

Name: Wayne Mark Rooney

Nickname: Roonaldo, Wazza

Date and place of birth: 24 October 1985, Croxteth, Liverpool, United Kingdom

Clubs: Everton (England) 2002-2004, Manchester United (England) 2004-present

Position: Striker

Early promise: At 17, Rooney became the youngest player to play for England. He earned his first cap in a friendly against Australia on 12 February 2003, becoming the youngest player to score an England goal.

World Cup appearances: Rooney broke a bone in his foot in April 2006, and looked as though he would miss the 2006 World Cup. But the England team doctors speeded up his recovery by making him sleep in an oxygen tent to help the bones heal more quickly. He came on as a substitute against Trinidad and Tobago, and started the next match against Sweden, but never looked fully match fit. He was red carded in the next game, which was England's quarter final defeat to Portugal.

Other international achievements: Rooney has looked sharp and hungry during England's 2010 World Cup qualifying matches under manager Fabio Capello. His two goals against Andorra in June 2009 meant he became the first person since Gary Lineker in 1991 to score 10 England goals in a season.

Something you might not know about him: Rooney's favourite band, The Stereophonics, performed at his wedding reception.

Become an international: Rooney is strong, quick, and shoots well with both feet. But what makes him really special is his will to win. He is an inspiration to his team and leads from the front.

The striker fights for the ball against Ecuador at World Cup 2006. England won the game 1-0.

Wayne Rooney's footballing career has always been special. His first Premier League goal, scored against Arsenal when he was only 16, was a 25-yard rocket that made him the Premier League's youngest ever goal scorer and ended the North London club's 30-match unbeaten run.

At 17, he became the youngest person to play for England, and the youngest player to score an England goal. At 18, he moved from Everton to Manchester United for £25.6m, the highest price ever paid for a teenager. And at UEFA Euro 2004 he became the youngest goal scorer in competition history, scoring two goals against Switzerland.

Rooney's success on the pitch has made him one of Britain's highest paid footballers. He has endorsement deals with Nike, Coca-Cola and Nokia, and has appeared on five straight covers of the FIFA video game series. He is married to his childhood sweetheart Coleen, whom he met when they were both in their final year of secondary school. In March 2006 he signed a huge £5m book deal to produce five books over a 12-year period, starting with an autobiography published after the World Cup 2006 and a teenage annual for the Christmas market.

Rooney was England's most dangerous striker during the UEFA Euro 2004, scoring in victories over Switzerland and Croatia, but during the quarter-final match against Portugal he broke a bone in his foot and had to be substituted. England lost the game on penalties. Then in April 2006, just two months before the World Cup Finals, he again suffered a foot injury that threatened to stop him playing in the tournament. Incredibly, he recovered in just six weeks, and was able to play in England's early group games but was shown a red card in the quarter-final against Portugal, which England lost on penalties. Under new England manager Fabio Capello, Rooney is back to full fitness and has played some of his best ever games for his country. He finished as England's leading goal scorer in the World Cup qualifying rounds for South Africa with nine goals.

Rooney – and England – are hoping for a great World Cup 2010.

"Wayne has a wonderful appetite for the game. You wish every player had that same appetite and desire to play. It's a joy to see a lad with that natural desire and enthusiasm."

Alex Ferguson in the *Daily Mirror*, February 2008

Fernando Torres

The complete striker

Torres has quickly become a hero for Liverpool fans.

"My job is to score goals. I want to win more titles and be the most important player in Europe and the world."

Torres, after his country's victory in Euro 2008, http://news.bbc.co.uk

Name: Fernando José Torres Sanz

Nickname: El Niño (The Kid)

Date and place of birth: 20 March 1984, Madrid, Spain

Clubs: Atlético Madrid (Spain) 2001-2007, Liverpool (England) 2007-present

Position: Striker

Early promise: Torres' international career got off to a winning start with Spain Under-16s at the 2001 Algarve Tournament. He also won the UEFA European Under-16s Championship the same year, scoring the only goal in the final against France, and finishing as the tournament's top scorer. In 2002 he won the UEFA European Under-19s Championship and was named Player of the Tournament.

World Cup appearances: Torres scored seven goals in 11 appearances in the World Cup 2006 qualifying rounds, including his first international hat-trick. He scored his first ever goal at a World Cup with a spectacular volley in a 4-0 win against Ukraine. In the second round he finished the tournament as Spain's joint top scorer alongside fellow striker David Villa.

Other international achievements: The youngest player to score for his full national side, Torres has already scored over 20 goals for his country. In Spain's UEFA Euro 2008 Final win, he scored the only goal in the 1-0 victory over Germany and was named Man of the Match.

Something you might not know about him: Torres started his football career as a goalkeeper before moving to striker.

Become an international: Torres has speed, power and great ball control. He often runs straight at defenders and dares them to stop him!

The Spaniard scores from the penalty spot against Tunisia at World Cup 2006.

For Spain, Torres plays alongside a group of the most gifted players that his country has seen for generations. Midfielders Cesc Fabregas, Andres Iniesta and Xavi Hernandez, and striker David Villa to name just a few. Spain are number 2 in the FIFA World Rankings after Brazil, and Torres is an outstanding member of this great team.

He has represented Spain at every level from Under-15 to Under-21. He was Spain's top scorer in the 2006 FIFA World Cup qualifying rounds, with seven goals in 11 appearances and continued his goal-scoring form with three more in the tournament. At UEFA 2008 he scored the match-winning goal in the final against Germany. This was Spain's first victory at a major tournament in 44 years.

Fernando Torres loves a challenge. At his first club Atlético Madrid he made his first team debut at 17, was the club captain at 19 (earning himself the nickname 'The Kid'), and was the team's top scorer for five seasons in a row. He turned down transfer offers from richer, more glamorous clubs, including Real Madrid, and instead stayed loyal to Real's smaller (and poorer) neighbour.

When he finally left Atlético for Liverpool in summer 2007 in a £20m deal, Torres became the most expensive Spaniard in the Premier League. He was given the club's number 9 shirt – worn by dozens of great goal scorers before him – and has exceeded everyone's expectations.

In his first season he managed 29 goals, at one stage scoring in eight consecutive games to equal the club record. He quickly became Liverpool's new cult hero and was even included in a list of 'The 50 Greatest Liverpool players' by *The Times* newspaper after just two seasons with the club.

Thanks to his performances at UEFA 2008, Torres was shortlisted for FIFA World Player of the Year 2008, and came third behind Cristiano Ronaldo and Lionel Messi.

Niggling injuries, including a recurring hamstring problem, have restricted Torres' appearances in Spain's 2010 World Cup qualifying campaign but no one doubts that he is capable of making a huge impact for his country in South Africa.

"Torres is a great player... He can go anywhere because he has really extraordinary speed and he knows how to dribble. There is no doubt he can be one of the best players in the world."

Luis Aragones (Spain's coach), after Euro 2008

Fabio Cannavaro

The world's best defender

Cannavaro shares a joke with Italian reporters after his country's 1-0 win against Australia at World Cup 2006.

"I feel like a typical Neapolitan because I like to enjoy life. We are a city with a lot of problems, but the approach to life is still happy. We try to live each day to its best and have a smile on our face."

Cannavaro, *Sunday Times*, September 2006

Name: Fabio Cannavaro

Nickname: Il Muro di Berlino (The Berlin Wall)

Date and place of birth: 13 September 1973, Naples, Italy

Clubs: Napoli (Italy) 1992-1995, Parma (Italy) 1995-2002, Internazionale (Italy) 2002-2004, Juventus (Italy) 2004-2006, Real Madrid (Spain) 2006-2009, Juventus (Italy) 2009-present

Position: Central defender

Early promise: Cannavaro won European Under-21 Championships in 1994 and 1996 and also competed at the 1996 Olympic Games in Atlanta, USA. He made his full international debut in January 1997 against Northern Ireland and has since played over 120 times for his country.

World Cup appearances: He has played in three World Cups, 1998, 2002 and 2006. He took over the captaincy from defender Paolo Maldini after the 2002 World Cup, and lifted the trophy as captain on 9 July 2006, the night of his 100th Italian cap. He was also crowned FIFA World Player of the Year.

Other international achievements: Cannavaro scored his first international goal on 30 May 2004 against Tunisia. In a 2009 Confederations Cup match against Brazil, he equalled Paolo Maldini's record of being Italy's most capped player. Along with goalkeeper Gianluigi Buffon he has played every game of Italy's 2010 World Cup qualifying campaign.

Something you might not know about him: Defending runs in the family. Cannavaro's younger brother Paolo is also a defender.

Become an international: At just over 5ft 7in, Cannavaro is short for a central defender but has the speed and strength of a sprinter, and is strong enough to stand up to attackers running at him!

One of the world's most talented defenders, Fabio Cannavaro began his career at Bagnoli before being spotted by scouts from Napoli. He went from ball boy for the great Napoli team led by Diego Maradona, to playing alongside his idols in the first team. He made his debut in March 1993 against Juventus in Turin. Financial problems forced Napoli to sell Cannavaro to Parma in 1995 where he won the UEFA Cup, the Italian Cup and Serie A (the Italian league) Defender of the Year.

Cannavaro made his debut for Italy in January 1997, and played his first international tournament at the 1998 World Cup, alongside legendary defender and mentor Paolo Maldini. Maldini's father Cesare was the Italian coach at the time. Cannavaro performed strongly, but Italy lost in the quarter-finals to France in a penalty shoot-out. At the 2002 World Cup, Italy was knocked out in the second round to a 'golden goal' from tournament co-hosts South Korea.

After the 2002 World Cup, Maldini retired and Cannavaro took over the Italian captaincy. He quickly won the team's wholehearted support, leading by example and always showing 100% commitment. He captained Italy throughout the 2006 World Cup qualifying campaign, and during the tournament he was given the added responsibility of holding the Italian defence together after an injury to his partner, central defender Allesandro Nesta.

One of Cannavaro's key performances came against hosts Germany in the semi-finals. His perfectly timed tackles prevented at least two certain German goals, and one interception and quick-thinking pass led to Italy's extra-time winner. He seemed to keep Germany out of the game single-handed. Along with goalkeeper Gianluigi Buffon, Cannavaro played every minute of every game in the 2006 World Cup and did not receive a single yellow or red card during the entire 690 minutes. He was runner-up for the Golden Ball for Player of the Tournament behind Zinedine Zidane, and made the tournament's all-star team, alongside six of his Italian team mates.

As long as he stays free of injury, Cannavaro plans to captain his country again at the 2010 World Cup. Italian hopes will again rest on his broad shoulders.

The World Cup-winning captain lifts the trophy after Italy beat France in the 2006 final.

"Germany 2006 didn't unearth any great talents. Only one player was brilliant from start to finish and that was Fabio Cannavaro."

Diego Maradona

Zinedine Zidane

The legendary craftsman

Zidane, a former Real Madrid player, is now a special advisor to the club.

"I was lucky to come out of a difficult area. It teaches you not just about football but also life. People had to struggle to get through the day. Football was the easy part."

Zidane, on his background, to *The Observer*, 2004

Name: Zinedine Yazid Zidane

Nickname: Zizou, ZZ

Date and place of birth: 23 June 1972, Marseilles, France

Clubs: Cannes (France) 1988-1992, Bordeaux (France) 1992-1996, Juventus (Italy) 1996-2001, Real Madrid (Spain) 2001-2006

Position: Attacking midfielder

Early promise: Zidane played his first game for France in a friendly against the Czech Republic in 1994, scoring twice. From then on, he became a regular in the French team.

World Cup appearances: Zidane won the 1998 World Cup, scoring two headed goals in the final against Brazil. Injury restricted his play in the 2002 Finals, and France was knocked out early. He retired from international football in 2004, but was persuaded to return as captain for the 2006 World Cup. Zidane was awarded the Golden Ball for Player of the Tournament.

Other international achievements: Following World Cup success in 1998, the French also won UEFA Euro 2000, becoming the first team since West Germany in 1974 to hold both the World Cup and the European Championships at the same time. Zidane was awarded his 100th cap for France in May 2006, being only the fourth French player in history to achieve this honour.

Something you might not know about him: Zidane didn't score a professional hat-trick until 2006, his final season before retirement.

Become an international: Zidane was one of the most skilful players in the game. He had the vision to see the best passes and the ability to make them happen.

Born on a tough Marseilles housing estate to poor Algerian immigrant parents, Zinedine Zidane became one of France's most famous and talented footballers. His passing skills, vision and often spectacular goals helped France win the 1998 World Cup, and later reach the 2006 World Cup Final.

Zidane played for some of the best teams in Europe, including Juventus in Italy and Real Madrid in Spain.

France won the 1998 World Cup Final 3-0 against Brazil, with two first-half headers from Zidane. Winning the World Cup in their own country made the French players national heroes. The team were even given medals by the French President.

Zinedine Zidane's footballing success continued with France winning the UEFA Euro 2000 final 2-1 against Italy. In 2001 he moved from Juventus to Real Madrid for a world-record fee of 78 million Euros (at that time worth £45 million). A year later in 2002 he won the UEFA Champions League for the first time, scoring the match-winning goal.

The Frenchman jumps clear of two Spanish players during World Cup 2006. France won the game 3-1.

Zidane's final World Cup in 2006 ended unhappily. France lost on penalties to Italy in the final, and Zidane was sent off for head-butting an Italian defender. However, he was still awarded the Golden Ball for Player of the Tournament. He also scored in the final, becoming only the fourth man to score in two different World Cup Finals.

Zidane retired from football in 2006 but still works behind the scenes at Real Madrid as a special advisor to the club's president. Two of his sons also play for Real Madrid youth teams. He was a true international great.

He played in four UEFA Champions League finals, and won the FIFA World Player of the Year award an amazing three times. Like all great players, he was able to raise his game at big tournaments, and make important contributions to his team when they needed him most.

Zidane's opportunity to play for his country came in 1995 when midfielder Eric Cantona was banned from the international game for one year for assaulting a fan. Zidane was given the chance to fill Cantona's position, and from then on was one of the first names on the team sheet for every game.

"Zidane has an internal vision. He can make the ball do whatever he wants. But it is his drive which takes him forward. He is 100 per cent football."

Aimé Jacquet (the former French manager), *The Guardian*, 2004

Ronaldo

The goal machine

Ronaldo celebrates after scoring a goal against Japan during World Cup 2006 in Germany.

"When I was a child I was poor and hungry but I liked what I did. It's still the same game I loved when I was a boy. When I am on the field... it is joy, pure joy."

Ronaldo, to *Details* magazine, 1998

Name: Ronaldo Luís Nazário de Lima

Nickname: The Phenomenon

Date and place of birth: 18 September 1976, Rio de Janeiro, Brazil

Clubs: Cruzeiro (Brazil) 1993-1994, PSV Eindhoven (Holland) 1994-1996, Barcelona (Spain) 1996-1997, Internazionale (Italy) 1997-2002, Real Madrid (Spain) 2002-2007, AC Milan (Italy) 2007-2008, Corinthians (Brazil) 2009-present

Position: Centre forward

Early promise: Ronaldo played his first game for Brazil in 1994 against Argentina. At 17, he went to the 1994 World Cup but did not play. He won a bronze medal at the 1996 Olympics.

World Cup appearances: Ronaldo has been in two World Cup-winning squads in 1994 and 2002, and lost in the 1998 final to France. In 2002 he won the Golden Boot for tournament top scorer with eight goals, including two in the final against Germany. He is only the second player (along with German Jurgen Klinsmann) to score three goals in three different World Cups.

Other international achievements: Ronaldo was included in Pelé's FIFA top 100 – a list of the greatest players ever.

Something you might not know about him: In the 1996 Olympics Ronaldo had the name 'Ronaldinho' (little Ronaldo) on his shirt. This was because defender Ronaldo Guiaro, who was two years older than him, was one of his team mates.

Become an international: As a boy, Ronaldo was a regular player of the South American sport of *futsal* – a fast, skilful game of 5-a-side football played with a small, heavy ball that helps develop passing skills and ball control.

The Brazilian striker became the World Cup's all-time top scorer with 15 goals when he scored here against Ghana.

Many people believe Ronaldo is the best striker in the history of football. His shooting accuracy, strength and ball control have made him the idol of other great players from Fernando Torres to Cristiano Ronaldo. The excitement he brought to the game increased television audiences around the world, and persuaded huge sports companies like Nike to invest more money in the game.

Practically a goal-scoring machine, Ronaldo averaged nearly a goal per game at his peak (in the 1996-97 season with Barcelona he scored 47 times in just 49 appearances). In four World Cup Finals from 1994 to 2006 he scored 15 times, and is the highest goal scorer in the history of the tournament.

But Ronaldo's first World Cup Final in 1998 caused newspaper headlines for what happened off the pitch rather than on it. The night before the final, he had an epileptic fit and was dropped from the team. Then, just before the game, he was brought back into the starting line-up. He played for most of the match, but performed badly and could not stop his team from losing 3-0.

Four years later, Ronaldo had a much more successful tournament. Brazil won a record fifth World Cup and Ronaldo scored twice in the final against Germany. He also won the Golden Boot as the tournament's top scorer with an amazing achievement of eight goals.

After the World Cup, Ronaldo moved to Spain and scored 23 goals in his first season for Real Madrid. His team won La Liga (the Spanish league title). Along with Frenchman Zinedine Zidane, Ronaldo has won three FIFA World Player of the Year awards in 1996, 1997 and 2002. He was the youngest player ever to win the award.

Although he has suffered several career-threatening knee injuries Ronaldo has always worked hard to recover and come back to football. He has played 97 times for Brazil, scoring 62 goals. He now plays for Brazilian club Corinthians, and is still as entertaining and as newsworthy as he has always been.

"It's not possible to stop a player like Ronaldo for 90 minutes."

Legendary German defender Franz Beckenbauer, after the World Cup Final, 2002

Pelé

First football superstar

Though Pelé ended his career in the United States, playing for New York Cosmos, he is still a key figure in the sporting world.

"I was born for soccer, just as Beethoven was born for music."

Pelé
http://www.football-rumours.com/pelé.html

Name: Edison Arantes do Nascimento

Nickname: Pelé

Date and place of birth: 23 October 1940, Três Corações, Brazil

Clubs: Santos (Brazil) 1956-1974, New York Cosmos (USA) 1975-1976

Position: Inside striker, playmaker

Early promise: Pelé made his debut for Santos at 15 years old. In his first full season, at 16, he became the league's top scorer and made such an impact that he was called up for Brazil. Pelé scored his first international goal aged 16 years and 9 months – the youngest player to score in international football.

World Cup appearances: Pelé won his first World Cup in 1958 at 17. He was the youngest player at the tournament and scored six goals in four matches. In 1962 and 1966, his play was restricted by injury although he did score in both tournaments. In 1970 Pelé was on great form, scoring four goals, including one in the 4-1 final victory against Italy.

Other international achievements: He is the Brazilian team's all-time leading scorer with 77 goals in 92 games. He retired from international football at a relatively young 31. With Pelé in the team, Brazil won 67 games, drew 14 and only lost 11.

Something you might not know about him: The nickname Pelé started as a joke because he could never pronounce the name of his favourite player Bile correctly.

Become an international: Pelé had great ball control and a powerful shot. His quick thinking – including shots from the halfway line, and dummies around the goalkeeper – helped him create opportunities that other players would not have seen.

The striker turns away in joy after scoring in the 1970 World Cup Final against Italy.

A great goal scorer, a strong leader, and an all-round team player, Pelé was the world's first football superstar. He always played with passion, skill and vision, producing moments of brilliance that are still remembered today. He won three World Cups in 1958, 1962 and 1970. He also captained the 1970 side that people say was 'the greatest team of all time'.

The son of a footballer, Pelé grew up in poverty and couldn't even afford a proper ball. He practised his skills with a grapefruit, or a sock stuffed with newspaper and tied with string. His abilities were soon spotted by a former Brazilian international player Waldemar de Brito who took Pelé to the local boys' club Baquinho, and then on to professional club Santos in São Paulo. He started playing for the Santos first team in 1956 and stayed there until 1974 – an amazing 18 years, scoring over 1,000 goals.

Just 10 months after turning professional Pelé made his debut for Brazil. His first World Cup in 1958 was a series of incredible achievements for such a young player. He was the youngest ever World Cup goal scorer, the youngest player to score a World Cup hat-trick (against France in the semi-final) and the youngest player to play in a World Cup Final, scoring two goals in Brazil's 5-2 win over Sweden. His first goal, a chip over the last defender and then a volley into the net, was recently chosen as one of the best World Cup goals in the history of the tournament.

After the 1962 World Cup, several European clubs including Real Madrid and Manchester United tried to sign him, but the Brazilian government declared Pelé an 'official national treasure' to prevent him being transferred.

Pelé's goal-scoring record is amazing – he scored five goals in a game six times, four goals in a game 30 times, and three goals in a game 90 times. He scored an amazing 1,282 career goals in just 1,363 matches. In the 1958 season alone, he scored 139 times. The records Pelé set will never be broken.

"I told myself before the game, he's made of skin and bones just like everyone else – but I was wrong."

Tarcisio Burgnich, the Italian defender who played against Pelé in the 1970 World Cup Final
http://espn.go.com/classic/biography/s/Pelé.html

Other World Cup Footballers

David Beckham
Beckham is probably the most famous football player on the planet, with his face on magazine covers and his name on millions of replica shirts. Born David Robert Joseph Beckham on 2 May 1975 in Leytonstone, London, he made his international debut at 21, and now holds the record for being England's most capped outfield player.

His first England appearance came in a World Cup qualifier against Moldova in 1996. He played in all the qualifying matches for the 1998 World Cup, and was included in England's squad for the tournament in France. He scored his first World Cup goal with a trademark long-range free kick against Colombia, but in the next game was sent off for a foul on Argentinian player Diego Simone. Reduced to ten men, England lost the game on penalties.

Facing heavy criticism from England fans, Becks worked hard to win back fans' loyalty with a series of match-winning performances, and in November 2000 he became England captain. It was his free kick against Greece in October 2001 that took England through to the 2002 World Cup Finals, and at the tournament he scored a winning penalty against Argentina. England lost in the quarter finals to eventual winners Brazil. Beckham's third World Cup in 2006 ended unhappily, with the team losing on penalties to Portugal. However, Beckham's determination to keep playing at the highest level means that he has remained a regular squad member for England's successful 2010 World Cup qualifying campaign.

Bobby Moore
The only England captain ever to lift a World Cup, Robert Frederick Chelsea Moore (12 April 1941-24 February 1993) was a vital member of England's World Cup-winning team in 1966. He is thought by many to be England's greatest ever defender. A skilful, intelligent player who anticipated opponents' moves and who 'read' the game better than any defender before or since, Moore played 109 times for his country. He also captained England a record 90 times. He began his England career in 1960 as part of the Under-23 squad, and won his first full cap in the 1962 World Cup Finals in Chile, South America. Moore played in all of England's games until they lost to eventual winners Brazil in the quarter-finals. On 29 May 1962, at just 22 years old, he captained his country for the first time. He was the youngest man ever to hold this honour.

Moore's greatest moment on a football pitch came in 1966 when England won the World Cup Final 4-2 against Germany. Moore set up the first goal for Geoff Hurst from a quickly taken free kick, and the fourth goal, again for Hurst, with just seconds of the match remaining with a perfect 40-yard pass to the striker's feet. Moore and his team mates became national heroes. He won the 1966 BBC Sports Personality of the Year award – the first footballer ever to win, and the only one for a further 24 years. He also received an OBE from the Queen. Moore played one further World Cup in Mexico 1970, and produced a confident and accomplished display against the eventual winners Brazil – including one interception against striker Jairzinho that is said to be 'the greatest tackle ever'.

Thierry Henry
A fast, skilful and high-scoring striker for club and country, Thierry Daniel Henry was born 17 August 1977 in Les Ulis, Essonne, a suburb of Paris. Henry's international career began in 1997 when he played for the French Under-20 side at the FIFA World Youth Championship,

alongside future team mates William Gallas and David Trezéguét. Later that year, Henry was called into the senior squad, where he made his debut in a 2-1 win over South Africa.

In 1998 Henry played in France's World Cup-winning squad and ended the tournament as his country's top scorer with three goals. He was a substitute in the final against Brazil, but didn't get on the pitch, because team mate Marcel Desailly's sending off reduced France to ten men. Henry was also a member of France's Euro 2000-winning squad, again scoring three goals and finishing as his country's top scorer. He was named Man of the Match in three of the games, including the final against Italy. A disappointing 2002 World Cup followed, as the team were eliminated in the group stages without scoring, and Henry was sent off in the second game against Uruguay. The 2006 World Cup was much more successful, with Henry scoring three goals and France reaching the final, which they lost on penalties to Italy. Henry is France's all-time leading goal scorer.

Diego Maradona

Diego Armando Maradona (born 30 October 1960 in Lanus, Buenos Aires, Argentina) is one of the most talented footballers the world has ever seen. His ball control, strength and amazing bursts of speed helped him beat defenders, set up goals for his team mates, and score them himself. In 91 games for Argentina he scored 34 goals, and set up many more for those around him. Football is a team game, and one superstar player does not usually guarantee success. However, without Maradona in their side, it is very unlikely that Argentina would have won the World Cup in 1986, or reached the final in 1990. He also led an unknown Napoli team to their only Italian league titles in 1988 and 1989.

But with Maradona, there were always bad headlines to go with the good. He is as well known for the illegal goal he scored with his hand against England in 1986 (which he called 'the hand of God') as he is for the fantastic second goal he scored in the same match. Picking up the ball in his own half, he beat five England players and the goalkeeper to score 'the goal of the century'. He was banned twice for failing drugs tests and suffered weight and health problems when he retired as a player. Outside football he worked as a successful chat show host in Argentina. He recently returned to the sport as a manager, and despite limited experience he is now in charge of the Argentinian national team.

Gianluigi Buffon

Quick, fearless, acrobatic and a great shot stopper, Gianluigi Buffon (born 28 January 1978 in Carrara, Italy) is currently the world's best goalkeeper. The Juventus Number 1 has been voted the Italian league's Goalkeeper of the Year seven times and World Goalkeeper of the Year four times.

'Gigi' won his first Italian cap at 19 – very young for a goalkeeper – in a 1998 World Cup play-off game against Russia. He was in the 1998 World Cup squad as back-up for first choice keeper Gianluca Pagliuca but did not play. Then an injury kept him out of Euro 2000. Buffon made up for these setbacks by winning the 2006 World Cup, keeping five clean sheets, and going 453 minutes without conceding a goal. The only times he was beaten in the whole tournament were an own goal from team mate Cristian Zaccardo against the United States, and a penalty from Frenchman Zinedine Zidane in the Final.

Buffon comes from a sporting family. His father was a weightlifter, his mother was an Italian discus champion, and his uncle played basketball. Buffon started his club career at Parma, and won the UEFA Cup and the Italian cup in 1999. Joining Juventus in 2001, he made an impact on the team, conceding just 23 goals in his first season. In 2006 Juventus were relegated to Serie B (Italian league second division) when club officials were found guilty of match-fixing, but Buffon stayed with the club and helped them win promotion back to Serie A the following season. He has played regularly in Italy's 2010 World Cup qualifying and is sure to be first choice for South Africa 2010.

Index

Argentina 6, 8, 9, 18, 22, 23
Arsenal 11
Australia 10, 14

Barcelona 8, 9, 18, 19
Beckham, David 4, 22
Best, George 4
Brazil 4, 6, 7, 8, 13, 16, 17, 18, 19, 20, 21, 22, 23
Buffon, Gianluigi 14, 15, 23

Cannavaro, Fabio 14-15
Cantona, Eric 4, 17
Capello, Fabio 10, 11
Champions League 5, 7, 9, 17

England 4, 5, 10, 11, 12, 13, 21, 22, 23
Everton 10, 11

Ferguson, Alex 4, 5, 11
FIFA 5, 6, 8, 9, 11, 13, 14, 17, 18, 19, 22
France 6, 8, 12, 15, 16, 17, 18, 21, 22, 23

Germany 12, 13, 15, 16, 18, 19, 22

Henry, Thierry 22, 23

Italy 6, 7, 14, 15, 16, 17, 18, 20, 21, 23

Juventus 14, 15, 16, 17, 23

Kaká 6, 7

Lineker, Gary 10
Liverpool 10, 12, 13

Maldini, Paolo 14, 15
Manchester United 4, 5, 10, 11, 21
Maradona, Diego 7, 8, 9, 15, 23
Messi, Lionel 5, 8-9, 13
Mexico 6, 9, 22
Milan 6, 7, 18
Moore, Bobby 22

Olympics 4, 8, 14, 18

Pelé 7, 18, 20-21
Portugal 4, 5, 10, 11, 22
Premier League 5, 11, 13

Quieroz, Carlos 4

Real Madrid 4, 5, 6, 13, 14, 16, 17, 18, 19, 21
red card 5, 10, 11, 15
Ronaldo 18-19
Ronaldo, Cristiano 4-5, 13, 19
Rooney, Wayne 4, 5, 10-11

São Paulo 6, 7, 21
South Africa 5, 9, 11, 13, 23
Spain 4, 5, 6, 8, 9, 12, 13, 14, 16, 17, 18, 19, 21

Torres, Fernando 12-13, 19
transfer fee 4, 5, 11, 13, 17

UEFA 4, 5, 7, 9, 11, 12, 13, 15, 16, 17, 23

Villa, David 12, 13

Zidane, Zinedine 15, 16-17, 19, 23

21st Century Lives

Contents of books in the series:

World Cup Footballers 978 07502 6201 9
Cristiano Ronaldo
Kaka
Lionel Messi
Wayne Rooney
Fernando Torres
Fabio Cannavaro
Zinedine Zidane
Ronaldo
Pele
Other World Cup Footballers

British Olympians 978 07502 5946 0
Rebecca Romero
Ben Ainslie
Rebecca Adlington
Lee Pearson
Sarah Storey
Chris Hoy
Eleanor Simmonds
Tim Brabants
Christine Ohuruogu
Other British Olympians

Reality TV Stars 978 07502 5690 2
Jordan
Leona Lewis
Ben Fogle
Cheryl Cole
Kelly Osbourne
Will Young
Myleene Klass
Lee Mead
Kerry Katona
Other Reality TV Stars

Teen Movie Stars 978 07502 5691 9
Zac Efron
Lindsay Lohan
Daniel Radcliffe & Emma Watson
Scarlett Johansson
Hilary Duff
Freddie Highmore
Christina Ricci
Thomas Sangster
Kirsten Dunst
Other Teen Movie Stars

Soap Stars 978 07502 5689 6
Ada Nicodemou
Jack P Shepherd
Kara Tointon
Kym Valentine
Lacey Turner
Roxanne Pallett
Patsy Palmer
Scott Maslen
Samia Smith
Other Soap Stars

Radio DJs 978 07502 5688 9
Chris Evans
Chris Moyles
Christian O'Connell
Jo Whiley
John Peel
Johnny Vaughan
Nihal
Sara Cox
Zane Lowe
Other Radio DJs

DJs and MCs 978 07502 5242 3
Fatboy Slim
Carl Cox
Paul Oakenfold
Missy Elliott
Judge Jules
Paul Van Dyk
Lady Sovereign
Eminem
P Diddy
Other DJs and MCs

Supermodels 978 07502 5243 0
Gisele Bundchen
Twiggy
Erin O'Connor
Alek Wek
Kate Moss
Marcus Schenkenberg
Tyra Banks
Lily Cole
Jamie Dornan
Other Supermodels

WAYLAND